Ali's Barbara

An Arabian Nightmare of a Minidrama

Richard Tydeman

A SAMUEL FRENCH ACTING EDITION

SAMUEL
FRENCH

FOUNDED 1830

SAMUELFRENCH-LONDON.CO.UK
SAMUELFRENCH.COM

CHARACTERS

in order of appearance

THE COMPERE
ALI, *of Baghdad*
BARBARA, *his daughter*
CASSIM, *Ali's brother*
FATIMA, *Cassim's chief wife*
JASMIN, *Cassim's second wife*
ZENA, *Cassim's third wife*
SARA, *Cassim's fourth wife*
FIRST MYSTERIOUS INTRUDER
SECOND MYSTERIOUS INTRUDER
THIRD MYSTERIOUS INTRUDER
Two or more SLAVES

SCENE: Ali's house in old Baghdad.

ALI'S BARBARA

The COMPERE, *in Eastern dress, appears in front of the curtain, bows to the audience, unrolls a large scroll in which a copy of the script is concealed, and begins:—*

COMPERE.
Once, long ago, in the far off days
When Arabian Nights were all the craze,
There lived in the city of old Baghdad
A bloke named Ali—a likeable lad;
He earned enough as a market porter
To keep himself and his motherless daughter,
The prettiest lass between Suez and Scarborough,
Known to her friends as Ali's Barbara.
Come then, to Ali's house with me,
As Barbara pours her dad some tea.

(Curtain rises. ALI *is reclining on a divan, while* BARBARA *pours him some tea which he drinks.* COMPERE *stands down* L.*)*

His meal complete, her father sighs
And looks his daughter in the eyes.

ALI.
My daughter, I have news to tell.

COMPERE.
To which the damsel answers,

BARBARA.
Well?

ALI.
Your Uncle Cassim wants to stay.

COMPERE.
The maid replies,

BARBARA.
That's spoilt my day.

ALI.
Why, don't you like your Uncle Cassim?

BARBARA.
If I could have my way, I'd gas him!

COMPERE.
Which statement makes it pretty clear
That Cassim's not a favourite here.

BARBARA.
His sneering ways just make me itch.
It's not our fault that we're not rich.

COMPERE.
But there's no time for any more,
For someone's knocking at the door.

(Knocking is heard. BARBARA *lowers her veil and opens door.)*

And from his carriage in the street
Steps Uncle Cassim with his suite.

(Enter CASSIM, *followed by four veiled wives.)*

With unctuous smile he turns to say,

CASSIM.
Well Ali, how's the world today?

COMPERE.
Then next his niece's hand he grabs:

CASSIM.   And how's my darling little Babs?

     (BARBARA *turns away in disgust.*)

COMPERE.   But Cassim's wives are looking daggers,
     And all of them are frightful naggers;
     So, following their mute instructions,
     Cassim proceeds to introductions.

CASSIM.   My chief wife Fatima you've met,
     And this is Jasmin, she's a pet;
     Zena and Sara, they're both new.
     Now come on, girls, say how d'you do.

FATIMA.   Dear Barbara, what a charming smile.
     (*Aside.*) Her clothes are all in last year's style.

JASMIN.   I've heard so much about you, dear.
     (*Aside.*) And most of it was true, I fear.

ZENA.   Pleased to meet you.

SARA.   Charmed, I'm sure.

ZENA AND SARA (*together, aside*). It must be awful to be poor.

COMPERE.   Now Barbara looks a bit askance—
     She's never had so many aunts.
     But quickly she regains the poise
     That every well-bred girl enjoys
     When facing this emergency
     And says,

BARBARA.   You'll have a cup of tea?

COMPERE.   They all say,

FOUR WIVES (*quickly*). Yes please!

COMPERE.   Like a shot.
     The journey's made them very hot;
     But ladies cannot lift their veils
     When in the company of males.
     So with the tea-pot and the tray,
     To Barbara's room they make their way,

  (BARBARA *goes out with tea tray, followed by the* FOUR WIVES.)

     And leave the men a little longer
     To quench their thirst with something stronger.

  (CASSIM *produces a bottle of whisky and fills the cups with it.* ALI *and* CASSIM *continue to drink during the next eight lines.*)

     Now just in case there's someone here
     Who thinks this story's rather queer,
     Allow me to explain a minute:
     The Forty Thieves do not come in it;
     For all this happened years before,

>In what are known as "days of yore":
>So with that word of explanation,
>I'll now get back to my narration.
>The bottle's less than quarter full,
>When Cass gives Ali's sleeve a pull,
>And asks him in a voice that wavers
>If he'll do some little favours.

CASSIM (*thickly*). The Tax Collector's on my tracks,
    So with me I've brought fifty sacks . . .

(*He mumbles into his cup of whisky.*)

COMPERE. But as he's whispering—in his cup, too!—
    I'd better tell you what he's up to.
    One sack is full of gold and loot,
    And forty-nine are packed with fruit.
    For Cassim, as the phone-book states,
    Retails bananas, figs and dates.

CASSIM. So be a jolly decent feller,
    And let me stuff them down your cellar.

COMPERE. Not used to such a lot of liquor,
    Ali's brain is muddled quicker;
    But giving Cassim's hand a squeeze
    He says:

ALI.   You stuff 'em where you please.

COMPERE. So fifty slaves with brawny backs
    Bring in the heavy bulging sacks.

(*A* SLAVE *enters carrying a sack and goes out immediately on the same side. A* SECOND SLAVE *enters with another sack and follows the first one off. Only two slaves are necessary, and they continue to enter and go out in turn—or they can walk round and round a screen—until the curtain falls. If they can have large numbers attached to their sacks, starting with "one" and working upwards each time they enter, so much the better.*)

>But though they make the work seem light,
>It looks like going on all night.
>Still, I suppose they've got to do it,
>So I suggest we leave them to it,
>And see what's happening to Babs.

(*Calling into the wings.*)

Right-ho then, William, close the tabs.

(CURTAIN *falls, leaving* COMPERE *outside.*)

>Now from the world of man's rough din,
>We turn to matters feminine,
>And join the ladies as they wait
>In Barbara's boudoir, tête à tête.

So please be quiet; don't make a clatter,
Or else you'll miss the gentle chatter
Of ladies' voices calm and still.
Please raise the curtain softly, Bill.

(The CURTAIN *rises. The divan has gone, and in its place is a window. This can either be a proper eastern window opening or just a clothes horse, standing on two chairs, with a sheet draped over the lower half. There are rugs and teacups on the floor.* FATIMA *and* JASMIN *are sitting;* ZENA *and* SARA *are standing. All are without veils. They argue raucously.)*

ZENA. It is!

SARA. It isn't!

JASMIN. Oh sit down!

ZENA. I'll bet you.

SARA. How much?

ZENA. Half a crown—
It's permed.

SARA. It's not; they're natural curls.

JASMIN. You're both wrong.

FATIMA. Oh be quiet, girls!
We can't discuss our niece's hair—
Especially when she isn't there.

COMPERE. What's this? The visitors alone?
(We've landed in a Danger Zone!)
Why isn't Babs upon her rug?

JASMIN *(turning)*. She's gone to fill the water jug.

(Enter BARBARA *with hot water jug.)*

BARBARA. I'm sorry I've been rather long.
How do you like it? Weak or strong?

COMPERE. So peace is now restored once more.
And sitting down upon the floor,
They all resume their proper station
And join in pleasant conversation.
But while they gaily drink their tea,
Behind their backs they do not see
Three stealthy figures softly creeping,
And through the window rudely peeping.

(Enter, crawling, three men of fearsome aspect, who get behind the window and pop their heads up over the sill one at a time.)

Three dirty double-dealers dashing;
Their double-crossing eyes aflashing.

Three double-barrelled names they carry—
Tom-tom, Dik-dik and Harri-harri.

(*The men's heads disappear.*)

Now Cassim's spouses, one by one,
Worn out by travelling in the sun,
Contentedly their eyes are closing,
And very soon all four are dozing.

(*The wives all sleep.*)

Then Barbara rises from the floor,
But scarcely has she reached the door,

(*As* BARBARA *reaches door,* TOM-TOM'S *head appears at the window.*)

When from the window comes the sound
Of :—

TOM.   Psst!

COMPERE.   And quickly turning round,
She strangles back a cry of fright
At such an unexpected sight.

TOM.   Oh shrink not, maiden, in alarm,
We do not wish you any harm.

DIK (*popping up in the window*). We all do really high-class jobs.

HARRI (*popping up between them with a fiendish grin*).
That's right. We only murder nobs.

(TOM-TOM *and* DIK-DIK *quickly thrust him down out of sight.*)

COMPERE.   But Barbara's puzzled by these three;
She's in the dark—and so are we,
Until the leader starts explaining,
And soon her confidence he's gaining.

TOM.   You see we go from door to door,
And rob the rich to pay the poor.

DIK.   When wealthy men we find, we woo them.

HARRI (*popping up between them*).
And if they won't pay up, we *do* them!

(*He draws a finger across his neck and makes a horrid noise with his throat. The others thrust him down.*)

TOM.   We hear that Cassim's near at hand,
With fifty sacks of contraband.

DIK.   If you can help us find this wizard,

HARRI (*thrusting the other two down as he pops up brandishing an enormous knife.*) We'll cut his throat from crop to gizzard!

(TOM-TOM *and* DIK-DIK *pull him down and reappear.*)

DIK.   Please take no notice of our friend,
He's definitely round the bend.

TOM.   Well, will you help us in our quest?

COMPERE.   Babs thinks; and then—

BARBARA.   I'll do my best.

COMPERE.   Now Uncle Cassim's met his match,
For Barbara starts her plans to hatch.
She tells the three to come tonight,
And knowing Cassim's short of sight,
She says:—

BARBARA.   Just do your hair in curls,
And come disguised as dancing girls.

TOM.   Oh what a plan!

DIK.   But s'pose it fails?

HARRI (*popping up between them and speaking in a cissy voice*).
I've come without my seven veils.

(*He ducks as if expecting the others to turn on him, but they take no notice.*)

COMPERE.   But now the sleeping wives awake,
So noiselessly their leave they take,
And whisper:—

TOM (*whispering*).   Till tonight.

DIK (*whispering*).   Farewell.

HARRI (*loudly*). We're going to give old Cassim — — —

(*The other two put their hands over his mouth and drag him off. The wives are now awake.*)

COMPERE.   Well!
The ladies view Babs with suspicion,
Until she makes the bold admission:

BARBARA.   Tonight we're going to have a party.

COMPERE.   They all rejoice with cheerings hearty.
Then suddenly they stop and stare.

JASMIN.   We haven't got a *thing* to wear!

COMPERE.   But isn't that, O husbands pray,
What married ladies *always* say?
So pull the curtain, let them go
And occupy an hour or so
With paint and powder, brush and file.
The curtains, William!

(CURTAIN *falls*.)

That's the style.
Now sinks the blazing sun to rest,
And darkness creeps from east to west.
The golden mantle of the day
Is folded up and put away;
And as the daylight hours are done,
The stars come peeping, one by one.
You realise of course that I'm
Just filling in a little time,
And improvising in between,
To let our stage-hands set the scene.
The silver moon with radiance bright
Is shining through the velvet night.
I hope they'll speed their preparation,
I'm running out of inspiration!

(*Turning towards curtain.*)

You're ready? Right. Then on we go
To see the last act of our show.

(CURTAIN *rises as on first scene.* BARBARA *is sitting between* ALI *and* CASSIM *on the divan. The wives are sitting on the floor, two on either side. The* SLAVES *are serving fruit and wine.*)

The shades of night have fallen fast,
And supper time is nearly past.
The wine is flowing like a river—
And Cassim's got a touch of liver.

(CASSIM *gives a hiccup.*)

But watchful Babs is wide awake,
And keeps her eyes on Dad's intake.

(SLAVE *goes to fill* ALI'S *cup, but* BARBARA *intervenes.*)

Then comes the moment she's expecting,
When Cassim, all his thoughts collecting,
Claps his hands and loudly yells:—

CASSIM (*clapping twice*). Bring in the Dancing Gels!

COMPERE.   Then amid sounds of girlish glee,
             Emerge our enterprising three.

(*Enter* TOM-TOM, DIK-DIK *and* HARRI-HARRI, *disguised as dancing girls. They perform an outlandish, eastern dance. At the end the others all clap.*)

             Says Ali, as his guests applaud:

ALI.   Ask what you please as your reward.

COMPERE.   Without delay the leading dancer
             Turns in a flash and gives an answer
             As quick as aeroplane's propeller:

Tom.	We'd like one sack from down your cellar.
Ali.	I can't go back upon my word.
Compere.	But poor old Cassim hasn't heard.

The three rush off to choose their sack,

(Exeunt the three, running.)

And presently they hurry back,

(They re-enter, running, with sack.)

And dump the sack upon the floor;

(They drop sack which obviously contains metal.)

Then Cassim wakes up with a roar:

Cassim.	You can't have that! It's one of mine.
Tom.	And all the other forty-nine?
Cassim.	Yes, yes.
Compere.	Disguise is at an end.

(The three throw off disguises.)

The three accusing strangers bend,
With outstretched fingers.

Tom. How d'you do?
We're from the Inland Revenue.

Dik.	Now kindly pay the tax you owe,
Harri.	Or into dungeons dark you go.

(Cassim swoons.)

Compere. But wasted are the words they say,
For Cassim's fainted clean away.

Fatima. Oh sirs, my husband's very poor—
And five can't live as cheap as four.

Jasmin. Have pity on his starving wives,

Zena and Sara *(together)*. And we will love you all our lives.

Compere. At this display of female favour,
Dik-Dik and Harri-Harri waver.

(Cassim recovers.)

Dik. Look here, Tom-Tom, it may be rash,
But wives would be more fun than cash.

Harri. I vote that Cassim we release,
And settle for a wife apiece.

Compere. At this arrangement Cass connives,

(Cassim clutches his sack, nodding.)

He'd rather have hard cash than wives.

(DIK-DIK *takes* ZENA *down* L. HARRI-HARRI *takes* SARA *down* R.)

The other wives to Tom-Tom run.

FATIMA AND JASMIN (*together*). Will you have both of us, or one?

COMPERE. But Tom-Tom pushes both aside;
He has in mind another bride.
And turning now to Ali's daughter,
With glowing words he starts to court her.
For though he seeks for tax collectable,
Yet really he is quite respectable.

TOM. I am Sultan of Avabanana.
Sweet Babs, will you be my Sultana?

COMPERE. The maiden blushes, gives a start,
And then says:

BARBARA. Yes, with all my heart.

ALI. Hey, just a minute, Sultan, sir,
I cannot manage without her.
If you take Babs, what *shall* I do?

CASSIM. Have one of mine; I've still got tw

(*So* ALI *takes* JASMIN, *leaving* FATIMA *for* CASSIM.)

COMPERE. So thus we solve a tricky question
Without hard words or indigestion.
We've paired them off, and just in time—
The way they do in pantomime.
It's time to draw the curtain now,
So forward please, and take your bow.

(*They come forward in couples, bow and step back again.*)

The moral of our little show
Is obvious to all, I know:—
You husbands, have you noisy wives?
And do they aggravate your lives,
And wear the trousers in your shacks?
Then pay them as your Income Tax!
Send every hen who is a pecker
To the Chancellor of the Exchequer.
Thus all your troubles will come right;
And we wish you a Good—Arabian—Night.

CURTAIN

www.ingramcontent.com/pod-product-compliance
Ingram Content Group UK Ltd.
Pitfield, Milton Keynes, MK11 3LW, UK
UKHW021818150726
7214IPUK00017B/185